David had packed his car the previous night for his return to Dartmouth. At about 9:15 on Monday morning he drove out of the driveway, honked the horn twice, and was gone from us forever . . . on this earth.

Sometimes MOUNTAINS MOVE

Sometimes MOUNTAINS MOVE

C. Everett Koop and Elizabeth Koop

ZondervanPublishingHouse
Grand Rapids, Michigan

A Division of HarperCollins*Publishers*

SOMETIMES MOUNTAINS MOVE

A Revised Edition

Requests for information should be addressed to:
Zondervan Publishing House
Grand Rapids, Michigan 49530

Library of Congress Cataloging-in-Publication Data

Koop, C. Everett (Charles Everett), 1916–
Sometimes mountains move / C. Everett and Elizabeth Koop.
p. cm.
ISBN: 0-310-48672-6 (alk. paper)
1. Consolation. 2. Koop, David Charles Everett, 1947–1968. 3. Rock climbing accidents—White Mountains (N.H. and Me.) I. Koop, Elizabeth. II. Title.
BV4907.K66 1994 94-45041
248.8'6—dc20 CIP

Printed in the United States of America

95 96 97 98 99 00 /❖OP/ 9 8 7 6 5 4 3 2 1

In Memory of

David Charles Everett Koop

December 30, 1947–April 28, 1968

Contents

PREFACE

Our twenty-year-old son, David, died twenty-five years ago. Perhaps this anniversary is an appropriate occasion to see how the passage of time has tempered the experience that both shattered us and blessed us.

The loss of David as a dearly loved, vibrant member of our family has not diminished in any way, although the scar over the open wound of grief has removed the acute pain that seemed unbearable at first.

We put our thoughts concerning David's death on paper three months after he was killed in 1968. We did not publish these thoughts at that time because our children felt that the narrative made us look too special to God, although, that was indeed how we felt. Ten years later we published our story.

We wrote it not as another book about handling grief and despair following death, but to show the grace and tenderness of our sovereign God in taking a particular family through His particular plan for them. Not one of us emerged the same. It is said that one only grows deeply in tribulation and sorrow, and we found this to be true.

It is very easy to lean on superficial supports when things are going well, but the loss of a child causes one to grasp for help and comfort beyond what even close family and friends can give. After all, they are suffering the same shock and grief.

When David, died, we turned to the only One who could give us support, comfort, and the assurance that He does not make mistakes, that He had taken David for his own reasons, and that in His faithfulness He would sustain us and keep us. And He still does.

We have added two new closing chapters telling some of the things that have happened to our family as God has worked in their lives over the intervening years. When we first wrote our story, it was in hope that it would bring some measure of comfort to those who struggle to survive a similar loss. It was our only reason for writing. But, now, fifteen years later we realize how many people have benefited from reading our story even though they do not share our faith in Christ and did not lose a child. Perhaps it is because they are relieved to learn that in all of life's vicissitudes—big and small—that someone is in charge. We know it is the Lord.

The story begins on a Sunday evening in April. At that time our family consisted of our married son Allen and his wife, Mary Ellen, living in an apartment only a mile away while he worked on his doctorate in history; Norman, living at home while attending a college nearby; Betsy a high school junior living at home; and our third son, David, a junior at Dartmouth College in New Hampshire.

It was David's custom to call us at nine o'clock each Sunday evening to bring us up to date on his activities and to chat a bit with the various family members. With the return of spring to the north country, David spent every nice weekend rock climbing in the White Mountains of New Hampshire and would report his latest climbing adventures to us in his Sunday evening calls. On April 28 the telephone remained silent as nine o'clock came and went and his mother, particularly, began to feel uneasy as the next hour dragged by. Finally, at ten o'clock the phone rang, and both parents hurried eagerly to answer on separate extensions.

"Is this Dr. Koop?"

"Yes. It is."

"This is Dean Seymour at Dartmouth College."

"You have bad news for me."

"I'm afraid I do."

"Is it the worst?"

"The worst, David is dead. He was killed in a climbing accident on Mount Cannon this afternoon. You take care of your family and call me back when you can. Here's the number." This was the way we learned that the Lord had taken David.

ONE

It is almost impossible to set down in writing how we felt. Even as we try to do so now, there is a recurrence of that first awful numbness as well as of the actual physical pain our bodies endured as we let the words of the dean race through our minds over and over again. It was absolutely impossible that David was dead; yet we were assuring one another that this was indeed the case.

We four who were living at home actually clung to each other in disbelief, for comfort, and in an effort to sustain one another. Allen was immediately called; he and Mary Ellen had just returned from New York. Within five minutes, they were with us.

The first thing that we did was to gather in a

circle with Chick, David's father, leaning against the curve of the piano. We put our arms around one another, and we prayed. We don't remember the many things we asked for, but we all do remember the overwhelming, oppressive grief that we felt. And we recall Chick's asking the Lord aloud, if He, having taken David from us according to His perfect will, would please show us some of the things he would accomplish through David's death.

It was not long before a strange peace descended upon us. It was nothing of ourselves, and therefore had to be the peace of God "which transcends all understanding." It is qualitative, not quantitative. It is sufficient. It is there, abiding, despite the tears and frightful hurt.

How many times did we say to one another in those next hours: "I can't believe it!"? There is a sense of unreality about death, but the unreality is beyond description in a sudden death like David's. Even as we write of David now, and speak of his death, a portion of our mind says, "Don't forget to tell David when he comes home that . . ."

When our disbelief finally gave way to the realization that we really knew nothing about the accident, Chick called the dean of the college.

ONE

These things were clear: David had been rock climbing with a close friend to whom he had been roped. The friend, Charlie Eriksson, was all right but in the hospital in a state of shock. The unbelievable news was that David had fallen at or shortly before noon. It seemed strange that we had all been living as usual all of those hours, while David lay dead on a cliff. The cause of his death was not known. The most awful thing was that his body was still on the face of the cliff.

It is hard to determine when acute grief becomes chronic. It is oppressive, even in sleep. The only time it is not felt is in the oblivion that comes from staying up so long that sleep comes upon reclining. There is no slow waking up out of the depths of sleep into the startling reality of grief, of hurt, of ache. You can see the same painful process going on in those about you; they feel it in you.

The grace of God made it possible for us to think, to act, and to ask questions. But who would have thought of the answers?

As we tried to piece it together, there were a number of things we didn't know.

How had David fallen?

Was there a failure of equipment?

Had he made a foolish mistake?

How had he died?

Did the fall kill him?

Did he say anything?

Why couldn't his body be brought down?

The *other* climber was down.

Had his friend come down alone, or had he been helped?

How long had David lived after the fall?

Who had seen David?

No one knew these answers except his climbing partner, Charlie Eriksson, who was in the hospital under sedation.

Then came the worst question of all: Was David really dead?

Our thoughts went back to some summers ago when two ill-equipped, inexperienced climbers were caught on a ledge on that same mountain. One died of injuries, and one of exposure, but not for a long, long time.

Chick has said since that even though (as time and facts contributed to our knowledge) he *knew* that David's body was broken—that it was clothed in climbing boots, climbing knickers, a red sweater, and a white helmet; and that rock-climbing equipment was fastened to his body—he always *thought* of David's body as lying motionless but whole, in grass, clothed in David's favorite costume: sneakers, old dungarees, and a striped jersey.

Our thoughts raced in circles. Perhaps he wasn't dead, but . . . but if not, then what a horrible situation—night on the mountain, temperature below freezing, survival almost impossible, and rescue even more impossible.

We'd have more details later, but apparently some rock had come loose and David had fallen; no one was quite clear on this. The rope had held, his partner had rappelled rapidly down to him, lowered David to a fourteen-inch sloping ledge and secured him to the face of the cliff, then climbed down to reach him.

Is the grace of God sufficient at a time like this and under these circumstances? Your gentle son, presumed dead, tied to the sheer face of a cliff hundreds of feet above the valley floor, the temperature below freezing, and the only person who could possibly shed any light on the matter lying under sedation in a hospital.

Yes, the grace of God was sufficient, and we knew a peace that did indeed surpass understanding.

TWO

Close friends whom we had called came to us immediately, and their distress over their helplessness gave us new insight into Christian love and concern.

Sleep came in the early hours of the morning only through physical and emotional exhaustion, but even in sleep, the oppressive weight of grief could be felt. Tears do *not* vanish in the morning. We can attest to the fact that on awakening there is first the knowledge that something is wrong, and then it comes quickly to our minds that David is gone. The horror of the details then come floating across our consciousness. Yet this is no contradiction to the theme of this testimony, that God is sovereign, even in the minute details of a death like David's.

The Bible does not tell us not to sorrow, but rather not to sorrow *as others do who have no hope.* If there were no grief or sorrow, no questions and doubts, how could God show His love, His sustaining power, and His close, intimate involvement in every affair of the lives of His children?

We have many friends and connections in New Hampshire. Allen's and David's relationship with Dartmouth College and the Appalachian Mountain Club, Norman's five summers on the Cog Railway at Mount Washington, and other contacts made over the past thirty years as we have summered in New Hampshire, brought us various bits of information, some accurate and some not. Eventually, we were able to talk with his climbing partner, Charlie, and slowly we pieced the puzzle together.

David and Charlie, his climbing partner, had decided to try a route up the rock face of Mount Cannon near Franconia Notch, called "Sam's Swan Song." While they hiked into the woods to the foot of the cliff, the weather was uncertain, but by the time they reached the starting point of the climb, the clouds had lifted, the pine needles were covered with rime ice, and the sun came out to make it one of those crisp, clear days in which David reveled.

The boys made their ascent by leapfrogging. One would climb a safe distance up and then fasten himself to the face of the cliff by means of a nylon rope tied into a piton (a steel spike with a ring on its end) driven into a crack in the rock by a hammer. Thus secured, he would say, "Off belay," meaning that he was safely over his immediate climb, anchored firmly to the rock, and now in a position to act as security for his partner. His partner would then climb from below, pass him, also secure himself and call, "Off belay." By noon, they had made a number of such leapfrog moves, and had stopped to reassess the route.

One of the many things precious to our family is the photographic record of all that David saw that morning, preserved in the camera in his knapsack. We can imagine his taking angle shots, first to the right and then to the left. David loved the exhilaration of "exposure," and his joy was to capture the sheer edge of the face of the cliff and then put it into perspective with another mountain in the background. At the lunchtime rest, David must have changed the film in his camera, because there were only two frames exposed on that roll—one showing Charlie on a ledge, examining the map of the rock face before the next ascent. Along with these pictures of that last day in David's life were others on the exposed film in his pack—but more of that later.

With Charlie fastened to the face of the cliff, David made his last climb up and then around an outcropping of rock, so that he was out of Charlie's vision. When sixty feet of nylon rope had been played out (the rope attached to one climber goes around the second climber's body so that, in case of a fall, the second climber can break the fall of his partner by using his body as a winch), David called, "Hey, Charlie. There's a piece of loose rock here, and it's as big as a house!"

We'll never know the details of the next few moments. David was a sophisticated climber, aware of the dangers of loose rock and of stone avalanches. Charlie heard a roar of falling stone, David fell, Charlie applied a dynamic belay, and David came to rest hanging sixty feet below Charlie.

Later, after a previous day's unsuccessful attempt by an army rock-climbing unit from Norwich University, an expert climber finally reached David's body. He later wrote: "He was about fifty feet above his belayer, Eriksson, without having as yet driven in any pitons or secured himself in any other manner. Thus, he was without any protection until he now placed a piton, a large angle-iron, under a large block at this highest point of his lead. He clipped in a bedayan carabiner, attached a sling, then a second bedayan, so that his rope was running nicely. Apparently, at this point the block commenced to slide, and he was aware enough to commence driving a second piton in another crack unconnected with the block, as an alternative measure. But he was never able to finish. The block slid out onto him and pulled him off, knocking him backward down the cliff. In its fall it completely smashed his left leg and knee."

The piton he drove into the rock marked with his code in colored tape was still there. It could have held his weight, so apparently the rock came loose next to him in the split second between driving the piton in and clipping himself to it.

What about the sovereignty of God? What if David had clipped in? We know that there are no "what ifs" or "if onlys" in God's plan. We believe that from the beginning of time God's plan called for David to climb—as an infant, as a boy, and as a man; to become expert at it; and to die in that particular, awful way—for a number of reasons that we think we can see, and probably for an infinite number we'll never have the human vision to understand.

Charlie got to David as rapidly as he could by rappelling as far as the rope would carry him (sliding in a sling passed between the legs and over the shoulder); and then, after fixing another piton, he descended to David, who hung a few feet above a fourteen-inch ledge. Charlie lowered David to this ledge and secured him there. David's left leg was crushed. Charlie applied a tourniquet above the injury, but the situation was already irreversible from blood loss.

David's first words were, "Off belay." While this signifies to us that David was confused (he had a hole in his helmet and a depressed fracture of his skull), it brings the comfort of suspecting that he perhaps had little knowledge of the gravity of the situation. But more than that, the Lord has used that phrase to comfort us when, in the sleepless hours of the night, our thoughts turned to the details of the fall. "Off belay" means to us that, under the circumstances of our son's life and his death, that he was secure, fastened to the Rock, and was then in no need of any other aid.

David also said, "It hurts," and a few moments later, "Charlie, you go down." Then he said, "I'm thirsty. It's hard to breathe," and finally, "I'm sleepy." And he closed his eyes.

How long did it take? Charlie estimates ten minutes. Chick rather thinks it was less than that. It must have seemed like an eternity to Charlie, perched with his battered friend on a fourteen-inch ledge, six hundred feet up the face of a cliff.

In addition to applying a tourniquet to David's bleeding leg, Charlie also tried mouth-to-mouth resuscitation . . . but all in vain. What a terrible ordeal for him! We hope he never forgets our profound gratitude for having done everything possible to save our son's life.

David bled to death, and from the nature of his injuries as well as from the symptoms David mentioned, the time could not have been long.

THREE

In grief, one seeks and finds comfort in situations that otherwise would be harrowing, if not unbearable. So we derived comfort from the knowledge that David bled to death—a quick, painless kind of death. Although he had other injuries, of which his crushed leg was the most severe, in his state of rapid exsanguination, he probably had little pain. What were his thoughts? Not clear ones, certainly, by the time that Charlie reached him. But he certainly knew of his predicament, during and after his fall.

Two other teams of two were on the rock face that day and saw the fall. They continued their climb to the top as rapidly as possible and then proceeded as fast as they could down the non-precipitous part of the mountain to report the fall.

It took the first rescue group and a physician, Dr. Harry McDade, some time to reach a place where voice contact with a bullhorn could be established with Charlie. From Charlie's description, the doctor knew David to be dead. Charlie then had to climb down the remaining several hundred feet of cliff and hike through the woods to the road. Therefore, David had been dead ten hours when the dean notified us. Some of this delay was because the dean wisely felt he must verify the facts before calling us.

Early Monday morning, the rescue party began the task of recovering David's body. We knew that David's body was the broken home in which he used to live. Yet, it was that body that had been David, and it was part of what we loved.

The rescue team, including their support, eventually comprised sixty-five men—New Hampshire Conservation officers, United States Forestry Service personnel, a crew from the Cannon Mountain Tramway, an Army ROTC rock-climbing unit from Norwich University, and half a dozen experienced rock climbers mostly from Massachusetts. The total time devoted to the work was 1200 man hours. The weather was poor, and we relayed a message through the courtesy of the editor of the *Manchester Union Leader* that we wanted no life to be risked in the attempt to remove a dead body. The first climbing group returned late that Monday without having reached David's body. They had climbed to within a few feet of his horizontal level but in a different vertical plane. The papers, television, and radio—especially in New England—were constantly repeating the failure. In the plan of God, David's mode of death received much publicity; so did the disappointing failure of recovery.

The second day's assault was led by Bill Putnam, an expert climber with extensive experience in the Himalayas and a member of the Appalachian Mountain Club. David's body was at the roadside at 4:30 Tuesday—fifty-two hours after he died.

Although the rescue process was harrowing and gruesome, God's grace kept us from seeing it that way. David was safe with the Lord. His body was a thing to be reckoned with, but when we thought of David, it wasn't as a crushed body roped to a cliff, exposed to driving rain and freezing temperatures. We remembered him as we had known him—vital, winsome, and agreeable; he was always in motion in our thoughts. Little threads of comfort again came to us through the account of a friend who witnessed the rescue. David's body was placed in a wire litter and lowered to the foot of the mountain by ropes. Then, two rows of thirty men lined up and passed David's body from one pair to the next down the last pitch. Not a word was spoken and David was handled as gently as if he were alive and to jar him would have hurt him.

Bill Putnam reported the accident in *Appalachia* for December 1968. Putnam is known to be critical of inexperienced climbers, of improper equipment, preparation, and plans. His report said in part:

I feel a high measure of respect for the two participants. They had all of the necessary equipment for the climb, and every item that could be felt desirable for any conceivable contingency; witness the fact that David's climbing-partner managed to come down under his own power. They had a spare rappel line. I went through Koop's pack and was quite impressed.

In summary, I find no reason to fault Koop or his climbing companion in any manner. . . . They were doing good work all the way according to witnesses whose competency I have good reason to trust.

He also wrote a personal letter to us, which concluded this way:

While I can give you no effective condolence or sympathy, you have my deepest respect, as did your son.

FOUR

With every painful step, the Lord provided a new comfort, and with each there was the opportunity to express a continuing faith in a God who makes no mistakes.

The late evenings of our days in waiting for David's body to be recovered became very precious. The immediate family, out-of-town family, and close friends would gather to read the many wonderful letters, to open the Scriptures together, to thank God for sustaining us, and to ask Him to show us something of the purpose of David's homegoing. We shed many tears as our initial shock was gradually displaced by the realization that David was gone from us. The tears flowed, not in bitterness but because of the deep, tender wound we felt as we understood that someone very precious would no longer be part of us here on earth.

We cannot honestly say that we felt a *perfect* peace at first; the circumstances surrounding David's death were too shocking and violent. However, we did experience a certain calmness and reassurance that surely came from the Holy Spirit. We knew that God had not deserted us nor forgotten us in our grief, but that He had taken our David to be with Him for a very real purpose. He wanted us to draw closer to Him—as a child clings to a parent, without questioning. This peace, is, and was, very real to each of us.

In the two days of waiting for the recovery of David's body, we were unable to make the usual funeral arrangements. We finally decided on a memorial service at our church rather than a funeral. Further, we by now acknowledged that David's body would never be fit for viewing, and with the children's agreement, we decided on cremation, without planning to look at David's body.

Then, when Betty, David's mother, realized that sixty-five men had spent forty-eight hours risking life and health to recover David's body, she said the least we could do was to look at him.

David's poor body was smashed—limbs, hands, and skull—but again, by a real miracle of God's grace, his face was in no way even scratched. Only the immediate family went to see him.

A memorial service was held for David in Rollins Chapel at Dartmouth College. The service closed with the organ's playing the Hallelujah Chorus, a piece that David played on the stereo all year round. It had no season for him. We had selected "Be Still My Soul" for the soloist in our own church, sung to the tune of Sibelius's "Finlandia"—the only music David himself played on the piano and organ.

The Philadelphia memorial service was at 4:30, and because of a traffic jam we were actually late to our own son's service. Confident that no funeral starts without the family, we entered the rear of the church, finding, to our dismay, that the service, through error, had indeed begun. But even this was, we are certain, in the plan of God.

We had wondered en route to the service if we might have made an unwise decision to hold it in so large a church, since the attendance would probably be small. Then, on arriving late and seeing the large church filled, we knew we had been led correctly.

As we entered, there was nothing to do but, at the close of the prayer, go down that long aisle and sit in the first two pews, which were reserved for the family. As it turned out, every eye was on us—we were in the spotlight as we could not have been had we slipped in quietly before the service began.

The entire service was a blessing to the family, an inspiration to the Christians present, and a clear exposition of the gospel of Jesus Christ, as well as the sovereignty and faithfulness of God, to the several hundred people present. Some of these people were coming in contact with a truly Christian service for the first time.

That night, while we contemplated the spectacle we must have seemed, tramping late down the aisle of that huge church, the phone rang and a minister from North Jersey told us: "I just wanted to say that to see a family walk down that aisle with heads erect, to see and hear them sing the hymns, and to see them walk out supporting one another but with heads held high, was a great testimony." Then we knew why we had been delayed in traffic.

FIVE

As those first long days and nights after David's death wore on, many of our children's friends came to our home—some having traveled a distance from their colleges and schools. The Lord gave wonderful and unusual opportunities for opening discussions on His sovereignty as well as the urgency for young people to accept Christ as their Savior and Lord. Sudden death at twenty is a shocking and sobering fact. It was both heartwarming and comforting for us to see our children gather with friends for such discussions, with Bibles opened, sharing an urgent message prompted by their experience.

Our children's grief was very deep, and they could not believe that life could ever be right or the same again without their brother. Of course, our family life never will be the same, but we are trusting in the Lord to help us accept the empty place in our family circle and to keep us constantly aware that David is in heaven—which is far better for him.

As parents, we have learned the uniqueness of our Heavenly Father's relationship with each of His children. It is true we still have our other children, and we are acutely aware of how precious they are to us, but the number of children in the family does not in any way diminish the uniqueness of the relationship between one child and his parent. This is the kind of close relationship and communication that God desires with each of us.

It is almost incomprehensible to our finite minds that, in His vast creation, God could be intensely, intimately concerned with one person—but this truth was made very clear to us through our pain when our physical relationship with David was severed. It was not by chance that the parent-child relationship developed. It was in the plan of God for each of us to know something of parenthood and sonship—that is, the closest expression of God's love for man—even His redeeming love.

FIVE

Because of the nature of David's death, the news traveled fast. Almost immediately messages and letters of sympathy began arriving. We stopped counting at one thousand. Many came from parents of Chick's small patients, and almost all of them seemed to cry out against the irony that Chick should lose his own son when he had saved the lives of so many children and had brought such comfort to so many during his twenty-two years as a children's surgeon. These letters almost demanded an answer to such unfairness, and Chick was able time and time again to emphasize and underline the sovereignty of God as he wrote . . . but now as a parent of a dead child rather than as a doctor speaking to grieving parents.

It appeared to be another piece in the puzzle of David's death—that a surgeon of Chick's wide experience and contacts with thousands of families should be the father of a child whose mode of death made such an impact on the public.

We shall never forget the blessing that our friends were to us during these difficult days. They were tireless in doing whatever they possibly could to help us or comfort us. One dear friend told us that for the first time she understood how the

Body of Christ suffers when one member suffers. We marveled that each in his or her own way showed us such love or brought us a special bit of comfort or reassurance of God's faithfulness.

SIX

As we look back over David's twenty years with us, we can see the long preparation David had for his final and fatal climb that Sunday afternoon on Cannon Mountain. From the time David started to crawl, he started to climb—out of his crib, up on furniture, up the stairs. At two years of age, his favorite activity was climbing the pine trees that separated our neighbor's home from ours. He would climb up to the second-story level and beyond, instinctively testing each branch for safety with his small foot, and then perch at the top, contentedly surveying the world below.

By the age of four, he had started to climb up on the roof of our three-story home, balancing himself easily as he walked along the ridge pole of the roof—to his great delight and his mother's horror. When forbidden to climb in one place, he would find another, always explaining to us that he was very careful and never took foolish chances. Indeed it seemed so, as he never fell, though he climbed everything in sight.

He was not only a sure-footed, skillful climber but also a "tumbler." One of the most frightening things David did when he was a teenager was to go to the peak of our three-story house for the amusement of his friends, appear to slip while walking along the ridge pole, and fall down the slanted roof, which brought him to the gutter just above the second-story windows. From there, he would fall about six feet to the roof of the porch, roll down about twelve feet, then off the edge of that to fall another eight feet to the ground. He did this skillfully, and without ever injuring himself.

During one summer while he worked as a brakeman on the Cog Railway at Mount Washington, he and some of his friends put on frequent sham accidents and fights for the amusement of the passengers. One of these consisted of waiting until all the passengers were in the car of the train on the summit, ready to make their descent from the mountain. Then, with the ringing of the bell that attracted their attention to the summit house, David would emerge, accidentally trip on the top step, and fall down the stairs into the cinders. This again, without ever hurting himself.

His staged fights on top of a coal bunker at the foot of the mountain frequently resulted in his falling from the top of the coal supply to the top of the coal tender and then to the ground. He had no fear either of climbing or of falling, and thoroughly enjoyed being a clown.

David's love for mountain climbing came in natural sequence, and he and his older brother together explored trails and peaks during summers in New Hampshire. How very natural and expected was his desire to go to college in New Hampshire.

Another evidence to us of the sovereignty of God in this matter is the fact that we never asked David not to climb. Had he asked us for a motorcycle, or had he asked us whether he might participate in certain other activities that have a definite risk, we certainly would have said, "No," or tried to talk him out of it. It never occurred to us to do this with his rock climbing, which seems quite unlike us. We really never understood the risk.

He started, very sensibly, taking instruction with small groups of rock climbers in the mountaineering club at Dartmouth and shared with us the fun and excitement it brought him. Even knowing his caution and conscientious planning for a climb, we would so often say, "David, are you being careful and not taking any foolish risks?" He explained in detail the method of rock climbing and the various safety factors provided—but, of course, he never mentioned the fact that *sometimes mountains move.* In letters we received from his rock climbing friends after his death, we were reassured many times that David was a careful and skillful climber, which to us was further proof that David's death was not due to an error in judgment, or an accident, but that God took David to be with Him right at the moment He wanted him and according to His perfect plan.

As we look back at the picture of David's life and preparation for his death at twenty years, we are made especially aware of God's guidance. David studied French for four years in high school, enjoyed it, and did quite well in it. The summer between high school and college, he was seeking some way to be with French-speaking people and at the same time to be in the mountains. Through an American friend working as a missionary in France, a most amazing summer was arranged for David. He was to spend the entire summer working in the French Alps at a camp run by Jeunesse Ardente, the French Young Life work. It proved to be a wonderful experience in every way. He became quite fluent in French; he hiked, climbed, and came to love the area around Taninges in the Haute Savoie. But most important of all, he came to understand the urgency of the gospel of Jesus Christ. He saw the change it brought about in young French lives, and he came into a close relationship with his Savior.

David's natural reticence kept him from revealing what we later discovered to be his fluency in French and the details of his commitment to Jesus Christ while working with Jeunesse Ardente.*

---

* Rodney and Fran Johnston, affiliated with The Evangelical Alliance Mission, and more recently with Young Life, were in charge of Jeunesse Ardente when David was in France. We are grateful to them for their friendship, for their support of David and all they have since done to make the David Koop Memorial a functioning reality.

SEVEN

As time went on, the Lord very graciously gave us several glimpses of the "big picture" in His plan. One can become so preoccupied with the acuteness or the uniqueness of his own grief that he can't see the forest for the trees. But God wonderfully expanded our vision on several occasions, like the zoom lens on a camera opening up the landscape behind a close-up scene. It is overwhelming to realize the length and breadth of the tapestry that God has woven around the lives of our family. David's death—the most enormous experience of our lives—was but one stitch in that tapestry, yet everything that happened in the lives of each of us was woven into the whole in such a way that many lines of stitches crossed at the moment of David's death. What an infinitesimal part of the design our lives are! Nevertheless, we are a part of the whole design.

We have often said since David died that if the preceding six months had been a scenario for a motion picture, the viewer could have said halfway through it, "David is going to die," so graciously had God placed David in special and privileged relationships to each of us.

The Christmas before his death, David had asked to spend half of his holiday in Louisiana in the home of the girl he loved. It wasn't easy to say yes to that request, since we saw so little of him, but how pleased we are now that David had that precious time with Lark, and that her family came to know him too.

At Christmas, David also decided to change his major from pre-med to geology, and his plans for graduate school leaned in the direction of the far west; so we were gradually becoming accustomed to the thought that we would be separated by a great distance and for long stretches of time. During spring vacation, we agreed that David would go directly from Dartmouth to his summer job on the Cog Railway at Mount Washington, in New Hampshire, with his brother Norman, and that he would spend three weeks at home after Labor Day before his senior year began. Do these seem like small things in God's graciousness to us? They are not! In times of grief such as we have felt, we grasp at anything for comfort, and it is reassuring to know that all those first summer months after his death, even if David were alive, he would not yet have been with us in our home.

The spring recess from college brought David home (four weeks before he died) for two weeks. It was an unusual time, a time we believe was wonderfully given to us by the Lord, and we cherish the memory now of the unique times we all had with David.

Allen and Mary Ellen lived only a mile away, and David and Norman lived at home, as did Betsy. Night after night they all sat up, long after their parents had gone to bed, talking of common interests. David wanted to go nowhere. He stayed home night and day, listening to the new stereo, and was commonly seen conducting an invisible orchestra in a magnificent crescendo. We heard snatches of his conversation with Norman as they discussed their previous summer and their next summer's activities on the Cog Railway. Norman was an engineer. David had been Norman's brakeman, and now he was to be his fireman. With Allen and Mary Ellen, his talk was of the ascent of a particular ravine, of the way the rime ice formed on the trees during a winter climb, or the way the lichens or the mosses grew on the rocks. Betsy's talk with him was of the French Young Life camp in the Alps at Praz-de-Lys, where David had spent a summer, and where Betsy intended to spend part of the summer of 1968.

David drove his grandmother to her home in Brooklyn after a visit with us, and Betty went along, providing a wonderful time for mother and son to be together on the return trip—an opportunity that had rarely been possible since David had grown up. On the trip, Betty spoke to David of her concern that as a geology major his strictly scientific instruction concerning the evolution of the earth might bring doubts and confusion over his faith and biblical belief. David reassured his mother that his faith in Jesus Christ was not in any way weakened by the apparent geologic age of the earth or existence of any prehistoric animal life. He said that he was having some difficulty resolving the incompatibility of biblical creation with geological evidence, but that his faith in the Atonement and the need for salvation were not in any way affected. How wonderful to recall these words a few weeks later.

Just before vacation ended, Chick had to go to New York for a professional meeting, and he asked David if he would like to drive. This was the first time David and his father had ever been away together alone overnight. It meant dinner, a movie, a night in a motel, a visit to a cruise ship to see some friends off to the Caribbean, a jaunt to Coney Island; but most of all, a day and a half of being together in the pleasure of each other's company, even at times without the spoken word.

The next Monday was the last time we saw David alive. He had packed his car the previous night for his return to Dartmouth, and at about 9:15 he drove out of the driveway, honked the horn twice, and was gone from us forever, on this earth.

Again the grace and the sovereignty of God combined to bring comfort to us at a later date. Chick had no surgery that morning, and therefore had stayed home from the hospital in order to be there when David left—an unusual set of circumstances. After the news of David's death, Chick clearly remembered that when David had driven off he had come into the house, looked out of the window, and prayed: "Dear Lord, David is Your child. Guide him and care for him according to Your will." And that prayer was answered.

EIGHT

In the fabric of God's plan there is one long, straight line of events that warrants narration. Chick had become experienced in dealing with the parents of dying children (and, of course, dead children) frequently in the course of his work as a child's surgeon, because the mortality is high in the two fields of endeavor in which he had developed special skills: cancer, and the surgery of the newborn.

After dealing with hundreds of parents concerning the impending death or the recent death of their child, one gets to the place where he almost believes that the quantity of experience is equal to going through the situation personally. When a youngster has cancer, the problems are most trying, because although the impending death is rather certainly known, it is not immediate, and in a sense, the parents lose the child twice—once when they are told of the poor prognosis and once again when the child actually dies. Over the years, Chick had developed a way of presenting this kind of news, and he frequently imparted his experience as best he could to younger surgeons in ward rounds, in seminars, and by lecture.

In the fall of 1967, at the end of a three-day graduate course in the surgery of childhood in Los Angeles, about five minutes before the close of the last session, someone asked, "What do you tell the parents of a dying child?"

It takes years of experience to feel confident in this area, and the knowledge cannot be transmitted in five minutes. Chick said to the panel faculty, "I'll take that," and for five minutes he rattled off the top of his head, giving advice on the subject. Someone in the audience took it down on a tape recorder, and shortly thereafter it appeared in a medical newspaper, *Medical Tribune.* That was seen by the editor of the *Bulletin of the American College of Surgeons,* and he asked Chick to adapt the material for a surgical audience. The *Reader's Digest* then asked for an interview on the subject, and in February 1968, an article appeared, "What I Tell a Dying Child's Parents," with Chick as the author. Chick tries never to talk about death without transmitting his faith in the sovereignty of God, and this was clearly evident in the *Reader's Digest* article.

At the Children's Hospital of Philadelphia, where Chick was Surgeon-in-Chief, there are physicians and surgeons who are preeminent in their particular specialties in the United States, if not in the world. Strangely enough, four such members of the staff have had a son or daughter with the very same rare defect or disease in which the father is an expert. This was common knowledge about the hospital, and is alluded to frequently, so it was natural for Chick to think, from time to time: "In what do I appear to be an expert?" Counseling about the death of a child was the obvious answer. The situation was intensified when a newspaper, the *Long Island Day*, published an interview with Chick on the subject of the dying child and his family, and also when Chick prepared two further manuscripts for *Medical Economics* and *House Physician* at the request of the editorial boards of those magazines.

The thought that he would lose a child

returned to Chick's mind frequently from early February through Good Friday of 1968. Quite unlike him, he did not share his disturbing thoughts with anyone. On Good Friday, Norman was late arriving from a trip to Boston, and communication had been misunderstood so that it appeared that Norman was overdue by four or five hours. Chick was certain that when the phone rang, it was the police reporting Norman's death. However, it was Norman himself. The anxiety over that event apparently wiped the thought of the possible loss of one of his children from Chick's mind, for he never thought of it again until the dean's phone call announcing David's death.

In all of these months, the Lord very graciously was preparing the whole family for David's loss. The response to the *Reader's Digest* article on the dying child was unexpected and overwhelming. Hundreds of letters came after the article was published, and many were long expositions on the matter of the loss of a child and the grief that follows. Most were from parents who laid their souls bare as they discussed the death of one of their own children, and all combined to expose us to an amazing variety of reactions to death, and of course, prepared us immeasurably as we agreed or disagreed. Many of these letters were read by Betty and the children. Even David, during his spring vacation, read a number of them. In retrospect, we can see the hand of a loving Heavenly Father giving each of us what amounts to a course in philosophy on the dying child. Inasmuch as the *Reader's Digest* article had emphasized Chick's faith in the sovereignty of God, this theme particularly was affirmed or refuted by those who wrote to us.

Chick can now attest to the fact that there is nothing in the world that comes anywhere near the experience of losing your own child. In a sense, Chick felt he was a better comfort to families whose child was dying before David was taken from us. Yet Betty feels that this is a purely subjective evaluation, because parents now know how well Chick can empathize with them. Perhaps part of Chick's feeling in this matter is that several times he has written on this subject and said that the physician should be all things to all men; the one thing the physician should not do is cry with the family. After David died, that was an emotional sign difficult for Chick to avoid when discussing the impending death of a child with the parents. Grief is indescribable and can be appreciated only by someone who has been through it in much the same way.

NINE

The central theme of our Christian understanding has always been the sovereignty of God. It is more than Romans 8:28. It is a firm belief that God makes no mistakes, doesn't change His mind, that things don't happen by chance, and there is no such thing as luck. Therefore, there can be no such thing as an "accident." The Lord never acts capriciously.

From the moment we gathered our children around us a few minutes after hearing of David's death, we have not asked "why?" in the sense that things might have been different "if only . . ." We believe that God never takes one of His children a minute before or a minute after He wants him. It was strange, therefore, to have so many people referring to "David's accident," and if now, in discussing his death, we too call it an accident, we are using the language of the world. His death had nothing to do with happenstance.

Suddenly we were faced with the necessity of practicing what we preached, or, as the gambler says, we had to "put our money where our mouth is." Through our grief, our faith in the sovereignty of God was not altered, and God could have left it that way. But instead, once more as a sign of His love and graciousness, God gave us assurance in so many ways that He is sovereign and that David's departure from us to be with Him was no mistake.

It has been the custom in our church for more than forty years to read a psalm each Sunday morning in consecutive fashion. If the psalm is particularly long, it might be divided into two or more sections for reading on consecutive Sundays. How often we have been impressed that this well-ordered, unchanging reading complements the Sunday school lesson, the pastor's sermon, or even a visiting preacher's message, when that individual could not possibly know of the "impending coincidence."

God also used this reading of the Psalms to demonstrate His sovereignty with reference to

David's death, beyond any shadow of a doubt. On the Sunday morning while David was climbing, just before his fall, we read the first half of Psalm 18. It spoke no particular message to us at that time. On the Sunday morning after David's fall, we read the second half of the psalm. Our first inkling that the Lord might be speaking to us through this psalm came in verse 27: "For thou wilt save the afflicted people" (KJV). We certainly were afflicted. And then, later in verse 30: "As for God, his way is perfect." We believed this, too, although it wasn't easy. Then came verse 33, and when we read, "He maketh my feet like hinds' feet, and setteth me upon my high places," the Word of God spoke to us of David. With verse 36, the sovereignty of God sounded forth as though it had been played on a trumpet: "Thou hast enlarged my steps under me, that my feet did not slip."

What could we do but sit in awe of the grace of God? David's feet did not slip! God took him. With understandable eagerness, we went back to the first half of the psalm, read the previous week, and there the Lord completed His message to us in verse 7: "Then the earth shook and trembled; the foundations also of the hills moved and were shaken. . . ." That was how David died. God shook the hill, and a piece of the cliff carried him to his death. His feet did not slip.

TEN

There is a wealth of Christian writing on the subject of chastisement, and these teachings can be very puzzling and disturbing to those going through tribulation. We have carefully considered Hebrews 12, on the subject of chastisement, and the nature of the word itself. Even after attempting to differentiate between chastisement and punishment, we have found that chastisement retains some of the idea of correction for something displeasing to God in our lives. We feel that in searching for such reasons for David's death, we would lose sight of the wonder of God's unfolding plan for our lives and for David's life.

We fully realize that there are things in our lives that are displeasing to God for which we could fairly expect chastisement. But to readily explain away our losing David by calling it chastisement could limit the entire experience. It would, of course, evoke a soul-searching for the reason behind the chastisement—a wondering why so many had to suffer for the special sin or sins of perhaps only one. Such a preoccupation with this dilemma would mean closing our eyes to the possibility that a death can be for a greater reason in God's plan.

God does not view physical death as we do; indeed, we are told that taking home to Himself one of His children is a precious thing to God and a cause for rejoicing in heaven. So, is it not possible that David's departure from this life and entrance into heaven occurred in the perfect time of God for His own purposes and to set into motion other plans and courses of action for those of us who remain here for a while longer?

In the aftermath of a violent death and the accompanying grief and hurt, it is very easy for anyone to ask, "Why are you doing this to me, God?" or "What have I done to deserve this terrible sorrow?" However, to wrestle with these thoughts is not only to search in vain for satisfactory answers; it also limits our openness to the far greater outworkings of God's sovereign plan.

If we can only look with expectation and trust at what God has planned through and around David's death, then we can see that the Lord does not fail us. He has already graciously shown us glimpses of some of the things He has planned, and we are comforted that His plan is best for us and best for David. We do not believe that David's death was chastisement or punishment. Sheer logic would make it hard to believe that a large family and close friends all needed chastisement at the same time, or that—if this were true—there weren't countless other families in need of the same thing. The twelfth chapter of Hebrews teaches a most important lesson on the Father's chastisement of his children, but Christians should be careful not to lump all affliction, tribulation, hardship, and sorrow under chastisement. To do so makes the time of trouble almost an endurance contest—with the reward that "therefore afterward it yieldeth the peaceable fruit of righteousness." In a sense, to accept chastisement as the only answer puts blinders on the one enduring the suffering, when in reality there may be far greater things being carried out in

God's plan through suffering. Indeed, the suffering may be just the natural consequence of an event in God's plan that is to have far greater impact than just the affliction of those hurt.

In the time of our trouble, it was the acts of God's graciousness to us as individuals and as a family that provided our greatest blessings. We cannot help but feel the Lord provided these cushions of comfort while he unfolded a bigger plan, far beyond the affliction of David's family. In an effort to be comforting, so many Christians glibly say, "God will fill the void." Instead, we found that the void is really never filled, but God does make the void *bearable.*

The many remarkable and cherished pictures we have of David during his last weeks on earth give us further reassurance that God's intricate plan was not chastisement, but that he was making David's absence as easy as possible for us.

After David's death, his father recalled that there was a roll of undeveloped film in David's own camera taken during David's spring vacation several weeks before. When developed, these pictures proved to be excellent and represented David dressed in his favorite outfit of a jersey, jeans, and sneakers, the way he usually was and the way we remembered him.

When David's college roommate came to Philadelphia for the memorial service, he brought with him the proofs of David's senior photographs, taken the spring of their junior year. They were exceptionally good and, amazingly enough, David had already made his own selection by marking the proof he planned to have finished. We were particularly touched when the photographer refused to accept payment, although we ordered many copies of several poses.

When David's girl, Lark, arrived at our home the day after his death, she brought with her a poster-size picture of David, two feet by three feet, which she herself had not as yet seen. Her mother had had it made from a slide and, after weeks of delay in the mail, it had arrived just before she flew to Philadelphia from Louisiana.

When she opened it, we cried but rejoiced through our tears as we saw David standing, completely relaxed, on the very peak of Mount Adams, his feet placed firmly on the rock, a pack on his back, hands at his sides, and his head and shoulders against a background of soft clouds. He truly looked as if he were only one step from heaven. This is the picture on the cover of this book.

When Lark returned to Louisiana, she found a letter from David waiting, which he had mailed just before his last climb. He had written: "This weekend Charlie Eriksson and I are going to do the longest and steepest route on Cannon, called Sam's Swan Song. This is the hardest route on Cannon. I have done all the easy ones, so I am ready to try the hardest one now. It's 800 vertical feet and is the longest rock climb in the east. It's a completely uninterrupted, vertical stretch of exfoliated slabs of granite. It should be a lot of fun. . . ."

The Lord even kept safe for us the roll of film in David's camera (although the camera itself was broken in his fall), as well as a finished roll in the pack on his back. These remarkable pictures show the course of his last climb, taken at different levels, and the last one taken of his climbing companion moments before he fell. These are painful pictures, in a sense, but we cherish them because of David's love of Cannon Mountain.

We went through David's slide box and came across picture after picture of Cannon Mountain taken over the years. It seemed to hold a special fascination for him and seemed a part of God's preparation for David's death on Cannon Mountain. It was not mere coincidence when we also realized that the picture taken of David at Dartmouth three years before, on his freshman outing club trip, showed him sitting on the edge of Mount Cannon's stone face, just a few feet from where he was to die, three years later.

ELEVEN

In the midst of our comfort in the sovereignty of God and His plan for David's life, we are perhaps most grateful of all for the knowledge that he is at this moment with the Lord. All of our children have made commitments to Jesus Christ, and we know that each one of them is assured of his or her eternal salvation, as are we. Yet it is strange that at that time, only in the case of David did we have evidence in writing of some of the things he felt. Are these not other little cushions of God's graciousness from which we can derive comfort and be grateful?

David had this to say in a section of an essay he wrote abut his experience in the French Alps:

This is, perhaps, the most beautiful spot I have been in. I received a new appreciation and realiza-

tion of the majesty of God's creation. There is so much variety and excitement. Sitting on top of the little hill behind the hotel, I'll try to describe the thoughts that went through my head. Looking down at my feet, there is a whole world of beauty in the Alpine flowers, the long green grass, and the rocks. Looking up just below the horizon, I can see hills and valleys, grazing pastures, and expanses of wooded areas with tall, thin, pointed fir trees.

Above the lowlands arise majestic rocky peaks, each peak so uniquely designed with its ridges, cols, and ravines. And still rising above them is the grandeur and splendor of the high, snow-covered Alpine peaks, with the massive white Mont Blanc rising up through the clouds and towering over all. The majesty of the view from my feet to the horizon makes me feel so insignificant, but I am comforted in the realization that I am a part of this magnificent creation and that God loves me, the most unworthy and imperfect aspect of the creation.

Later on, in a brief paragraph about spiritual benefits, he said this:

At first, my language barrier prevented me from profiting from the messages, Bible studies, and discussions (as much as I might). After a few weeks, I had satisfactory comprehension but was unable to con-

tribute much to the discussions or answer questions. But there was one event which lifted me spiritually and strengthened my relationship with the Lord. This happened suddenly while seeing the film Lucia, *presented at Taninges. When Billy Graham spoke, I could feel the presence of the Holy Spirit, and something stirred within me and I felt uplifted and very close to the Lord. I haven't lost that strengthening renewal of my relationship with my Savior.*

Once in a public speaking class at Dartmouth, David felt compelled to make his final presentation one of Christian witness and spoke about the fact that the fulfillment of biblical prophecy concerning Israel was proof enough that the Bible is the inspired Word of God. He also once took the occasion, in writing an English theme, to bear witness to his faith. He chose to compare some of the philosophy in Thoreau's *Walden* with the Atonement of Christ. He wrote:

Thoreau . . . speaks of man also as separating himself from winter and entering spring, separating himself from his sinful past and entering a new and redeemed life: "In a pleasant spring morning all men's sins are forgiven. Such a day is a truce to vice. While such a sun holds out to burn, the vilest sinner may return." Thoreau asks why men are still bonded to the past and to sin and why they don't accept "spring." He asks why men are not willing to forgive their fellowmen and to forget their evil past. His answer is that men do not accept God's free pardon and forgiveness for their own sins.

This idea is in direct accordance with the Christian concept of Christ's atonement for man's sins. God, having loved man in spite of the fact that "all have sinned and come short of the glory of God" (Romans 3:23), gave men the gift of atonement by sending His Son as a sacrifice to pay for the wages of sin, which is death. Any man who accepts this gift of love is justified through that, "As Christ was raised from the dead by the glory of the father, even so, we also should walk in newness of life" (Romans 6:4).

When David's Bible finally came into our hands, we read it with much interest and were amazed again by the fact that David's underlining of Scripture was unusual for a boy of twenty. Many of the things he had underlined turned out to be the very verses chosen by us to be used in his memorial service. It was not that he had a preoccupation with death, but he had assurance of justification and eternal life, based upon the resurrection of his Savior, Jesus Christ.

TWELVE

One of the most precious letters we received came from the mother of one of David's climbing friends at Dartmouth College. She stated that her son had phoned right after the accident, and when she had heard what he had to tell her, she must have said: "Oh, please stop climbing." Her son apparently went back to his room the same night that David died and wrote the following letter to his mother. This was never intended for us to see, and therefore it was all the more wonderful when she kindly sent it to us.

Your reaction was normal, for parents, I suppose. Still, you knew one of my friends just died, and you said, "Stop climbing." From your point of view, I can see this reaction; from mine, it makes little sense.

You never met Koop, so let me tell you a little about him. A twenty-year-old geology major, Dave was one of those few people who really impress you in the first few moments after meeting him. Immediately you wanted to strike up a friendship. He was totally selfless. I have never seen him do anything with his own benefit in mind. He had a warm, kind personality which made one immediately like him. That was one thing, but once you became one of his friends, well, I had had such a respect for very few people. His death came as quite a blow to me.

Dave and I had made great plans for this summer. Among other climbs, we were going to do Sam's Swan Song, the one where he died Sunday. _______ and I were looking forward to riding up the Cog Railroad with him, and everything was to be so great. He was the best friend a guy could ever have—in fact, I can remember distinctly as we went up Whitney-Gilman Trail, that he was too good *a person to be real. I actually breathed a sigh of relief when we got off the cliff, so worried was I that something would happen. It was almost a kind of worship. I can't believe that Dave is gone.*

I'm sure I have had some idea of how his family must feel—but you shouldn't try to discourage me *from climbing. It's something that gets into your blood. Unless you've done it, you cannot understand. There is far more than muscling your way up over a rock. First, there is the beauty of the outdoors—many know that. Then, there comes the almost mathematical approach. The route poses a problem—where are the holds that will permit one to surmount it? What movements give solution to the rock? There is a strange beauty of movement, a combination of dancing and gymnastics. There is a definite art in the performance of movement on a rock face: balance, so you don't fall, tricks with your hands and feet to permit ascent up an otherwise insurmountable wall.*

Besides the skill with which these movements are done, there is the fitness that must come too. One cannot stand on tiptoe for long without losing leg strength, and then the hands are quickly tired, so there is an art to the conservation of strength so that when the handholds give out, you can tiptoe across a narrow traverse on perfect balance and pull yourself over a wall when the footholds give out.

Then there is the solitary confrontation with one's self and nature. The leader thinks to himself as he moves—Can I combine strength with precision, balance with rhythm, and experience with the holds before me in order to get over this stretch of rock? *It is all these qualities molded together so that they are almost a religion (not a sport) that makes rock climbing the activity it is.*

Unfortunately, there is one quality you have no control over. You can develop strength, balance, rhythm, and the others with experience . . . sometimes a mountain may just not conform to your wishes; there may be a loose rock there that you don't know about until it comes loose. Nothing can control that. This we have to take into consideration when we climb, but if you have the urge to climb within you, if you can "feel" as a sixth sense the powers of balance, precision, strength, beauty, rhythm, and everything else, you have to overlook that factor (that sometimes mountains move*)—there is no other way.*

We loved David; he satisfied us in so many ways as a son, and we took the greatest pleasure in realizing that he knew of our satisfaction. Yet we believe that many times we underestimate the impact our children have upon others of their own age. David was so quiet in many circumstances that we little realized the friendships he had made, the lives he had influenced, and the number of people who had come to love him.

One of the hardest and yet most precious things in preparing this writing was for us to read the letters that David's friends wrote to us at the time of his death. From a grade-school-through-high-school friend came this:

I wish there were more I could do than just send this card to extend my deep respect, sorrow, and sincere feeling. My twelve years of friendship with David will always exist as a special kind of memory; and I know I will often stop and think about him. I don't think that the world deserves to go on without him. In my heart he will not be forgotten; his image will always be a monument in my memory for what he was.

A paragraph of a letter from one of David's Dartmouth friends touched us deeply in its simplicity:

Although I have known him not quite two years, I cannot help but share your grief and sense of loss. Dave and I were in several classes together. We joked, wrestled, and skied together. And he cut my hair.

Although David's brothers emptied his college room of his personal belongings shortly after he died, they kept his Bible on his desk in the hope that his friends, especially those for whom the Scriptures were opened at his memorial service, might read it (which some of them did).

It was ten weeks after David died when his Bible came into our hands. We had been told by his brothers that his bookmark was in Jude, and presumably this was the last Scripture passage he had read. David's Bible is a Revised Standard Version, and in that particular edition, the book of Jude ends on the left-hand page with only one verse, the last one. We opened his Bible and read the last thing that David had read: "And now unto him who is able to keep you from falling. . . ."

God was able, but in His sovereignty He chose not to.

THIRTEEN

We learned many spiritual lessons through David's death—some hard, some deeply reassuring. But we also learned some very practical things about the course of recovery after losing a loved one, and we feel they are worth mentioning:

- there is no timetable for grief
- there is no blueprint to show one the way through it
- each recovery is extremely personal
- the expectations of others should be ignored

Often Christians are too glib with their clichés to other Christians struggling to cope with overwhelming sorrow. The words *victory* or *joy* are not what a devastated parent wants to hear! A friend from a prominent Christian family, who had lost her son, felt somehow put on center stage to exhibit joy in what God had sent her to bear. But she was just a brokenhearted mother who at first hurt too much to fill expectations for other Christians. Her faith in God's sovereignty never wavered, but she had her own timetable for recovery.

We have two other friends who long after the death of their wives still take some measure of comfort in the sight of clothes in the closet, desks, and bureaus the way they had been, and kitchens maintained in the old familiar way. These men are not creating shrines. They are normal, functioning people, but they feel better and more comfortable with their wives' possessions in evidence. The stereotyped steps of recovery from grief, so glibly set forth, can cause guilt and fear of failing in many. *There is no timetable!*

The best way to help persons struggling to recover is to really listen, to feel comfortable with their tears, never to judge, to commend or praise for every step toward recovery, and to consistently point the hurting person to the Lord for the ultimate comfort and security.

There are so many wonderful reassuring Scripture passages to read with them:

> And we know that in all things God works for the good of those who love him, who have been called according to his purpose.
>
> Romans 8:28

> For I am convinced that neither death nor life, neither angels nor demons, neither the present nor the future, nor any powers, neither height nor depth, nor anything else in all creation will be able to separate us from the love of God that is in Christ Jesus our Lord.
>
> Romans. 8:38–39

> As for God, his way is perfect; the word of the Lord is flawless. He is a shield for all who take refuge in him.
>
> Psalm 18:30

> Never will I leave you; never will I forsake you.
>
> Hebrews 13:5

> In my Father's house are many rooms; if it were not so, I would have told you. I am going there to prepare a place for you.
>
> John 14:2

To him who is able to keep you from falling, and to present you before his glorious presence without fault and with great joy—to the only God our Savior be glory, majesty, power and authority, through Jesus Christ our Lord, before all ages, now and forevermore! Amen.

Jude 24–25

Too soon after a death, many people feel they should not mention the lost loved one to the bereaved person because they would somehow "remind" him or her of the terrible loss. How foolish! We found after David's death certain acquaintances and even friends would actually avoid us. They were no doubt afraid of upsetting us, although we would have been pleased that they remembered David, as we thought of little else and longed to talk about him.

It all takes time. So often, in Chick's dealing with families who have lost a child, friends and acquaintances—and even family members—have said such things as "It's been six months, she's got to snap out of it" or "It's been four months, he has to get on with his life."

The reality is that most parents never get over the loss of a child. There is no such thing as "snapping out of it," and even though they do eventually get on with their lives, they do so accompanied by a sense of loss and a very private grief.

The inevitable *what ifs* and *if onlys* always present a tremendous barrier to recovery. In every death there are agonizing thoughts of how death could have been avoided or at least postponed (delayed). But a firm belief in the absolute sovereignty of God is the *only* sure way to avoid the futility of dwelling on the *what ifs* and *if onlys.* These *must* be put behind the grieving person in order to recover! It takes great willpower to do this and a great determination to acknowledge that the plan of God leaves no room for such obstacles to healing. In our own case, we could have dwelt endlessly on the fact that we had not only supplied David with all of his rock-climbing gear but had encouraged him in what we thought to be a wholesome outdoor sport.

Our most agonizing *what if* and *if only* had to do with the cataclysmic change in the face of the cliff. David had already secured a piton in solid rock. It was found there later by those who recovered his body. How long would it have taken David to unclip his carabineer from his belt and clip it into the piton right before him? A few seconds at the outside. Had he been able to accomplish that simple task, the falling face of the cliff would have been but a brush with death rather than the cause of his death.

But how could *we* have thwarted the purpose of God in His plan to take David to Himself that day in April? In our absolute conviction of this truth, we were not retreating behind an empty comfort. Instead, we had the peace of mind that can come only from the assurance in the Scriptures. David had gained everything, and in that same plan we were included and not left comfortless.

FOURTEEN

Our children, Allen, Norman, and Betsy are now all in their forties. Each recovered at a different rate and in a different way from their brother's death. No doubt, the personality and the maturity of each accounted for the differences.

Betsy found herself most comfortable in her senior year of high school with her Christian *Young Life* friends, who were willing to listen when she talked about how much she missed David. They could understand how her belief in a God who doesn't make mistakes brought her comfort. Of course, at seventeen, the subject of death is remote and embarrassing to talk about for many.

The following summer, Betsy and a friend

returned to the Young Life camp in the French Alps, where the David Koop Memorial Chalet to house campers would eventually be built. She somehow wanted to round out David's experience there and to be with the French young people who had been his friends. She had a particular burden for Bruno, a boy who had been devoted to David and a close friend. She continued with him the Christian witness that David had begun.

A year later, Betsy entered Wheaton College in Illinois and thoroughly enjoyed her four years there. She met and married Gordon Thompson, a classmate, soon after graduation and we've often told him we could not have fashioned a better husband for our daughter. After a two-year stint in the army, Gordon started work with MAP International—a Christian relief agency whose work is mainly in the third world. He managed the Eastern Branch of MAP and Betsy ran Missionary Services until their children were born—Mark in 1977 and Karen in 1982. Since then she has been pleased to be a homemaker, feeling that keeping a Christ-centered home is her mission, being supportive to Gordon, and working with him bringing their small PCA mission church in Georgia to an organized church status. It is our delight that her beliefs are still centered in the sovereignty of God through lessons she learned so young and so well when her beloved brother was taken. Gordon recently moved to International Aid, Inc., a well-focused ministry of Christian health care throughout the deprived world, with headquarters in Michigan.

Allen's grief when David died was intense and immediate. Despite the four years between them, they had always been close, and David shared Allen's fascination with the mountains of New Hampshire. At a very young age, they had spent a week together hiking along the ridge of the presidential range from one Appalachian hut to the next. In fact, after his death, Allen was plagued by dreams of searching for David's body in those very mountains. He was never bitter but missed him so much. And still does.

Allen and his wife left Philadelphia a few weeks after David died and settled near Hanover, New Hampshire, where he was completing his independent study for his Ph.D. from the University of Pennsylvania in history. The urgency to share their vital faith with Dartmouth students led very soon to the establishment of a Bible study that Allen taught. At first, it was slow going, but by the fall, interest had picked up and continued to grow—some drawn to it because there was no other study like it on the campus. Some knew Allen as David's brother, and his classmates had been very affected by the impact of David's death. College students are not supposed to die, and such a death is an unwelcome reminder of mortality. Allen continued for several years to teach the class and eventually turned it over to others to lead as it became the Dartmouth Christian Fellowship—then the largest student organization on campus except the Dartmouth Outing Club.

Allen went on to be a history professor and at present is a visiting professor at Dartmouth when he is not deeply involved in his father's many-faceted career. His editorial skills have proven invaluable to Chick.

Although Allen is not ordained, he is a licensed minister in the state of New Hampshire, and he pastors two small churches not far from his home in New London. When they first asked him to become their pastor, he told them that he would preach each Sunday, but with his teaching and other academic obligations he could not assume the pastoral work. However, as he came to know and love the members of his two small flocks, he has indeed become their pastor in the full sense of the word. We love to hear him preach the Word of God faithfully and with the skills he has learned as a teacher.

His two daughters, Jennifer, now twenty-four, and Heather, twenty, followed him into a Dartmouth education, and he has passed on to them his interest in history and in the White Mountains of New Hampshire. But, most important, they are enthusiastic Christians whose lives reflect their abiding faith in Christ.

Even though our seven grandchildren never knew David, they all know the story of his life and death and how our family was drawn closer to one another and to the Lord at the time He kept us through our saddest hour. This book in its previous editions has been used by our older grandchildren as a Christian witness to their friends. And it has been instrumental in moving some to search the Scriptures.

Allen has also authored two books. His second book, *Stark Decency*, is a poignant story of the interaction between German prisoners of war and their guards in a little-known prison camp in Stark, New Hampshire during World War II. His first, *American Christians in Secular France—*

1945–1975 concerns the impact of American evangelical missionaries on post-war France, and is a primer for church growth in modern post-Christian Europe.

The story of Norman's odyssey from being a lackluster college student majoring in sociology to becoming a remarkable minister of the gospel has been the most startling result of David's death.

At first, Norman seemed unable to slow down enough to grieve in any depth for David. His already rapid pace just increased, and he immersed himself in every possible activity, saying to us, "We just have to keep going—we can't stop our lives even though David died." He was engaged to Anne at that time, and that summer we took both Anne and Norman with us to England on a trip we had already planned because Chick had some long-held obligations at the University of Liverpool. After the academic proceedings were over, we drove to the Lake District to spend a few days alone in the cottage of a friend. We arrived at dusk on a cold, dreary, rainy afternoon, and after laying in a few necessary supplies, Chick tried his hand at getting a coke fire going in the little stove. The atmosphere was cheerless at best, and we noticed that the usually effervescent

Norman was becoming quiet and withdrawn. As the evening wore on, Norman's grief for his brother finally began to surface. He broke down and was inconsolable as he cried for hours. We talked at length, but neither Anne nor we could comfort him. At last, he slept, and when he came downstairs the following morning, he was calm and quite himself again. He said to us, "Well, I've finally decided what I want to do with my life. I made a commitment to Christ a few years ago, but now I've really seen Him in action in our family as He took us through David's death, and I want to spend my life making Him known to others. I'm going to seminary."

Not only was this a profoundly startling statement to us but a real about-face for Norman. We were of course delighted but did wonder if his decision was only the result of the deep emotion he was finally giving way to in grieving for his brother. However, he never wavered in his decision. He rearranged his courses for his senior year in college to take the necessary prerequisites for seminary and then continued on for four more years until his ordination at the Tenth Presbyterian Church in Philadelphia where he had been associated since infancy. His first call in 1973 was to the historic Presbyterian church in Deerfield, New Jersey, where he remained for seventeen years. He was then called to perhaps the even more historic Congregational church in Woodstock, Vermont, "gathered" in 1773, where he still serves. We love to hear his strong, faithful, expository teaching—always rooted in the Scripture and always underscoring our most reassuring and favorite doctrine: the absolute sovereignty of God.

What more could we ask? And how abundantly we have been blessed! In an old hymn, "How Firm a Foundation," there is a line that reads, "I will sanctify to Thee Thy deepest distress." This is what the Lord did for each of us in a most remarkable way.